The Outcasts of Poker Flat

*Fate, Sacrifice & Unlikely Heroism
in a Snow-bound Sierra Settlement*

A Modern Translation
Adapted for the Contemporary Reader

Bret Harte

Translated by Tim Zengerink

Table of Contents

Preface Message to the Reader 1

Introduction 2

The Outcasts of Poker Flat 6

Miggles 21

Thank You For Reading 36

Preface
Message to the Reader

Rebuilding the Greatest Library in Human History

Thousands of years ago, the Library of Alexandria was the heart of global knowledge — a sanctuary where the wisdom of every known civilization was gathered and shared freely.

And then, it was lost.

Now, we're rebuilding it — and you are invited to join us.

At the Library of Alexandria, we've set out to make every book available to every person on Earth — not just in print, but in every language, every format, and for every reader.

Here's how we do it:

- **Deluxe Print Editions at True Printing Cost** - Order any book as a high-quality paperback, elegant hardcover, or stunning boxset — and only pay what it costs to print. No markups. No middlemen.
- **Unlimited Access to the Greatest Works** - Enjoy thousands of timeless classics — from Plato to Shakespeare to Tolstoy — in beautiful, modern eBook and audiobook editions. Read and listen without limits — for every reader, everywhere.
- **Modern Translations for Every Language & Dialect** - We're reimagining the classics in clear, accessible language — and translating them into every dialect imaginable. Everyone deserves to understand humanity's greatest ideas.

When you visit **LibraryofAlexandria.com**, you're not just accessing books — you're joining a global movement to restore, preserve, and share the wisdom of civilization.

Join us today at LibraryofAlexandria.com

Together, we'll ensure the light of human wisdom never fades again.

With gratitude,

The Modern Library of Alexandria Team

Visit:
www.libraryofalexandria.com
Or scan the code below:

1

Introduction

The Harsh Frontier and the Human Spirit

Bret Harte's *The Outcasts of Poker Flat* is a tale that transcends its Western setting, offering a powerful meditation on fate, morality, and the capacity for sacrifice in the face of adversity. First published in 1869, this story is among Harte's most celebrated works, not only for its vivid portrayal of frontier life but also for its deep emotional resonance. It is a narrative that challenges our assumptions about good and evil, exploring the complex humanity that lies beneath society's labels.

Set in a small mining settlement during the California Gold Rush, the story opens with a scene of judgment. A self-proclaimed committee of moral arbiters in Poker Flat decides to cleanse the town of those it deems undesirable—individuals who, for various reasons, do not conform to the rigid standards of respectability. Among these are John Oakhurst, a professional gambler known for his calm demeanor and sense of honor; the Duchess and Mother Shipton, women whose livelihoods are tied to the darker corners of society; and a thief named Uncle Billy. Banished from the town, these outcasts are forced to confront both the harsh elements of the Sierra Nevada mountains and the prejudices of the world that has cast them aside.

What makes Harte's narrative so compelling is his refusal to present these characters as one-dimensional villains or victims. Instead, he explores the nuances of their personalities, revealing unexpected virtues and moments of grace. The gambler, often regarded with suspicion, emerges as a figure of quiet nobility, while the women—initially seen through the lens of their social stigmas—prove to be capable of profound compassion and courage. In the crucible of isolation and impending disaster, these outcasts display a depth of character that challenges conventional notions of morality.

The snowstorm that traps the outcasts in the mountains serves as both a literal and symbolic test. It is in this harsh, indifferent environment that the true measure of their humanity is revealed. Stripped of societal roles and material possessions, they are left with only their instincts, their choices, and their capacity for selflessness. Harte's portrayal of their struggle is both tender and tragic, capturing the fragile beauty of human decency in the face of overwhelming odds.

Themes of Sacrifice, Redemption, and Fate

One of the central themes of *The Outcasts of Poker Flat* is the idea of redemption. Each character, in some way, is given an opportunity to transcend the circumstances of their past and to define themselves through their actions. Mother Shipton, for example, makes the ultimate sacrifice by quietly starving herself so that the young and innocent Piney Woods may have a better chance of survival. Her act of selflessness, set against the backdrop of a life often judged harshly by others, speaks volumes about the hidden depths of the human soul.

John Oakhurst, the gambler, is perhaps Harte's most complex creation in this story. Known for his skill at cards and his unshakable composure, Oakhurst reveals a code of honor that transcends the rough moral landscape of Poker

Flat. He cares for his companions, makes strategic decisions to ensure their safety, and ultimately faces his fate with a stoic dignity that marks him as a true hero. His final act, both somber and defiant, underscores Harte's meditation on fate—the idea that life, like a hand of cards, is often a mix of chance and choice, but that true character is shown in how one plays the hand they are dealt.

The juxtaposition of the outcasts with Tom Simson (the "Innocent") and Piney Woods adds another layer of meaning to the story. These two young lovers, untainted by the cynicism of the older characters, bring a sense of purity and hope to the group. Their presence softens the hardened outcasts, drawing out qualities of kindness, protection, and generosity that might otherwise have remained hidden. In this way, Harte suggests that redemption often comes not through wealth or social status but through the simple, human connections we forge with one another.

The snowstorm itself functions as a character in the narrative—a relentless, impartial force of nature that tests the limits of human endurance. It is a reminder of the unpredictability and indifference of the frontier environment, a landscape that both challenges and shapes those who inhabit it. Harte's descriptions of the snow-covered wilderness are as evocative as his character studies, creating a setting that is both beautiful and deadly, serene and merciless.

Bret Harte's Frontier Vision and Legacy

Bret Harte's genius lies in his ability to blend the rough realism of frontier life with moments of deep emotional truth. In *The Outcasts of Poker Flat*, he avoids romanticizing the West as a land of unmitigated heroism. Instead, he offers a more nuanced vision, one that acknowledges both the brutality and the humanity of those who lived on the margins of society. His characters are not idealized figures but flawed, complex individuals whose actions reveal the capacity for both vice and virtue.

Harte's style, often described as "local color," captures the unique atmosphere of the Gold Rush era while also speaking to universal themes. His dialogue, humor, and attention to detail bring the world of Poker Flat to life, while his exploration of loyalty, sacrifice, and moral ambiguity ensures that his stories remain relevant today. *The Outcasts of Poker Flat* is not just a story about the past; it is a timeless reflection on the resilience of the human spirit.

The enduring appeal of this story lies in its emotional honesty. Harte does not shy away from tragedy—the fates of the outcasts are harsh, and their heroism does not guarantee survival. Yet, in their final moments, there is a sense of dignity and grace that elevates them beyond their circumstances. It is this combination of realism and transcendence that has made *The Outcasts of Poker Flat* a cornerstone of American literature.

For modern readers, the story offers both entertainment and insight. It challenges us to look beyond surface judgments, to see the humanity in those who are marginalized or misunderstood, and to recognize that heroism often emerges in the unlikeliest of places. Harte's outcasts, though condemned by their society, leave behind a legacy of courage and selflessness that resonates far beyond the confines of Poker Flat.

The Outcasts of Poker Flat

As Mr. John Oakhurst, a gambler, walked onto the main street of Poker Flat on the morning of November twenty-third, 1850, he sensed that the town's moral climate had shifted since the night before. Two or three men who had been talking seriously together stopped their conversation when he came near and gave each other meaningful looks. There was a Sunday-like quiet hanging in the air that seemed threatening in a town not accustomed to the peaceful influence of the Sabbath.

Mr. Oakhurst's calm, handsome face showed little worry about these signs. Whether he was aware of any underlying reason was another matter. "I figure they're looking for someone," he thought to himself; "probably me." He put back in his pocket the handkerchief he had been using to brush the red dust of Poker Flat from his clean boots, and calmly dismissed any further speculation from his mind.

In truth, Poker Flat was "looking for someone to blame." The town had recently lost several thousand dollars, two prized horses, and a well-respected citizen. The community was going through a fit of moral outrage that was just as wild and uncontrolled as the very actions that had triggered it. A secret committee had decided to cleanse the town of all undesirable people. This goal was achieved permanently with two men who now hung from the branches of a sycamore tree in the ravine, and temporarily through the exile of certain other unwanted individuals. I'm sorry to report that some of these people were women. However, to be fair to their gender, I should mention that their misconduct was part of their profession, and it was only when dealing with such clearly defined forms of wrongdoing that Poker Flat dared to pass judgment.

Mr. Oakhurst was correct in assuming that he fell into this group. Several committee members had pushed for hanging him as a warning to others, and as a reliable way to recover from his pockets the money he had taken from them. "It goes against what's fair," said Jim Wheeler, "to let this young fellow from Roaring Camp—a complete outsider—walk away with our cash." However, a basic sense of fairness among those who had been lucky enough to win money from Mr. Oakhurst overrode this petty local bias.

Mr. Oakhurst accepted his sentence with philosophical calm, remaining composed even though he could sense his judges' uncertainty. He was too much of a gambler not to accept whatever fate dealt him. To him, life was nothing more than an unpredictable game, and he understood that the odds always favored the house.

A group of armed men escorted the banished troublemakers of Poker Flat to the edge of town. The exiled group included Mr. Oakhurst, who was known as a dangerously calm man and the main reason for the armed guard, along with a young woman commonly called the "Duchess," another woman who had earned the nickname "Mother Shipton," and "Uncle Billy," a suspected thief who stole from mining operations and a notorious drunk. The procession drew no remarks from onlookers, and the escort remained silent throughout the journey. When they finally reached the ravine that marked the farthest boundary of Poker Flat, the leader of the escort spoke briefly and directly to the point. The outcasts were warned never to return under threat of death.

As the escort vanished from sight, their bottled-up emotions burst forth in a few hysterical tears from the Duchess, some foul language from Mother Shipton, and a parting barrage of curses from Uncle Billy. Only the philosophical Oakhurst remained quiet. He calmly listened to Mother Shipton's desire to cut someone's heart out, to the Duchess's repeated declarations that she would die on the road, and to the shocking oaths that seemed to be jolted out of Uncle Billy as he rode ahead. With the easygoing good nature typical of his kind, he insisted on trading his own riding horse, "Five Spot," for the pitiful mule that the Duchess was riding. But even this gesture failed to bring the group any closer together. The young woman straightened her somewhat disheveled feathers with a weak, worn-out flirtatiousness; Mother Shipton glared at the owner of "Five Spot" with hatred, and Uncle Billy included the entire party in one sweeping curse.

The road to Sandy Bar—a camp that hadn't yet experienced the reforming influences of Poker Flat, and therefore seemed to offer some welcome to the outcasts— stretched over a steep mountain range. It required a full day of hard travel to reach. As the season was well advanced, the group quickly left behind the humid, mild climate of the foothills and entered the dry, cold, invigorating air of the Sierra Mountains. The path was narrow and challenging. At midday, the Duchess tumbled from her saddle onto the ground and announced she wouldn't go any further, forcing the party to stop.

The location was remarkably wild and striking. A forested amphitheater, enclosed on three sides by steep cliffs of bare granite, sloped gradually toward the edge of another cliff that looked out over the valley. It was, without question, the most appropriate place for a campsite, if camping had been wise. However, Mr. Oakhurst understood that barely half the trip to Sandy Bar had been completed, and the group lacked the equipment and supplies for any delay. He explained this reality to his companions bluntly, adding a philosophical observation about the foolishness of "giving up before the game was finished." Yet they had brought alcohol, which in this crisis served as a substitute for food, warmth, rest, and good judgment. Despite his objections, it wasn't long before they were all somewhat affected by it. Uncle Billy quickly shifted from an aggressive mood to a dazed one, the Duchess became overly sentimental, and Mother Shipton began snoring. Only Mr. Oakhurst remained upright, resting against a rock, quietly observing them all.

Mr. Oakhurst didn't drink. It got in the way of a job that demanded a cool head, emotional control, and sharp thinking, and as he put it himself, he "couldn't afford it." As he looked at his sleeping fellow outcasts, the isolation that came from his outcast profession, his way of life, and even his flaws weighed on him seriously for the first time. He busied himself brushing off his black clothes, washing his hands and face, and performing other tasks that reflected his carefully maintained neat appearance, and for a moment he forgot his irritation. The idea of abandoning his weaker and more pitiful companions probably never crossed his mind. Still, he couldn't help missing that thrill which, strangely enough, helped him maintain the steady composure he was famous for. He gazed at the dark walls that shot up a thousand feet straight above the circle of pine trees surrounding him; at the sky, filled with threatening clouds; at the valley below, already growing darker with shadows. As he did this, he suddenly heard someone call his name.

A horseman slowly climbed up the trail. Looking at the fresh, open face of this newcomer, Mr. Oakhurst recognized Tom Simson, who was also called the "Innocent" of Sandy Bar. He had encountered him several months earlier during a "little game," and had, with complete calmness, won the young man's entire fortune—which totaled about forty dollars—from that trusting youth. When the game ended, Mr. Oakhurst pulled the young gambler aside behind the door and spoke to him this way: "Tommy, you're a good kid, but you can't gamble to save your life. Don't attempt it again." He then gave him back his money, gently pushed him out of the room, and in doing so made Tom Simson completely devoted to him.

There was a trace of this in his youthful and eager greeting of Mr. Oakhurst. He had set out, he explained, to travel to Poker Flat to seek his fortune. "Alone?" No, not exactly alone; in fact (a giggle), he had eloped with Piney Woods. Didn't Mr. Oakhurst remember Piney? She who used to serve tables at the Temperance House? They had been engaged for a long time, but old Jake Woods had opposed the match, and so they had eloped, and were heading to Poker Flat to get married, and here they were. And they were exhausted, and how fortunate it was they had discovered a place to camp and found company. All this the Innocent shared rapidly, while Piney, a sturdy, attractive young woman of fifteen, appeared from behind the pine tree, where she had been blushing out of sight, and moved to her lover's side.

Mr. Oakhurst rarely bothered himself with emotions, and even less with what was proper; however, he had a sense that their situation wasn't good. Still, he kept his composure enough to kick Uncle Billy, who was about to speak, and Uncle Billy was alert enough to understand that Mr.

Oakhurst's kick represented a higher authority that wouldn't tolerate any nonsense. He then tried to convince Tom Simson not to delay any longer, but his efforts were useless. He even mentioned that they had no supplies or way to set up camp. Unfortunately, the Innocent countered this concern by telling the group that he had brought an extra mule carrying provisions and by finding a rough log cabin structure near the path. "Piney can stay with Mrs. Oakhurst," said the Innocent, gesturing toward the Duchess, "and I can take care of myself."

Only Mr. Oakhurst's warning foot prevented Uncle Billy from exploding into loud laughter. Even so, he felt he had to walk up the canyon until he could regain his composure. There he shared the joke with the tall pine trees, slapping his leg repeatedly, making faces, and cursing as usual. But when he came back to the group, he discovered them sitting around a fire—since the air had become unusually cold and the sky had clouded over—apparently having a friendly conversation. Piney was actually chatting in an eager, youthful way with the Duchess, who was listening with an interest and liveliness she hadn't displayed in many days. The Innocent was speaking enthusiastically, seemingly with equal success, to Mr. Oakhurst and Mother Shipton, who was actually becoming pleasant. "Is this supposed to be some damn picnic?" Uncle Billy thought with inner contempt as he looked at the woodland scene, the flickering firelight, and the tied-up animals nearby. Suddenly an idea mixed with the alcohol vapors clouding his mind. It was clearly meant to be funny, because he felt the urge to slap his leg again and shove his fist into his mouth.

As shadows slowly climbed up the mountainside, a gentle wind swayed the tops of the pine trees and whispered through their long, dark corridors. The damaged cabin, repaired and covered with pine branches, had been set aside for the women. When the lovers said goodbye, they naturally shared a kiss so genuine and heartfelt that its sound seemed to carry above the rustling pines. The fragile Duchess and the spiteful Mother Shipton were likely too shocked to comment on this final display of innocence, so they turned silently toward the shelter. The fire was built up again, the men settled down in front of the entrance, and within minutes they had fallen asleep.

Mr. Oakhurst slept lightly. As morning approached, he woke up numb and freezing. When he stirred the fading fire, the wind, which had grown fierce, carried something to his face that drained the color from it—snow!

He jumped up, planning to wake the sleeping people since there was no time to waste. But when he looked toward the place where Uncle Billy had been lying down, he discovered the man was gone. A sudden suspicion flashed through his mind and a curse came to his lips. He rushed to the area where the mules had been tied up; they were nowhere to be found. The tracks were already quickly vanishing in the snow.

The brief surge of excitement brought Mr. Oakhurst back to the fire with his characteristic composure. He chose not to wake those who were sleeping. The Innocent rested peacefully, wearing a smile on his cheerful, freckled face; the pure Piney lay sleeping next to her more delicate companions as serenely as if watched over by heavenly protectors; and Mr. Oakhurst, pulling his blanket around his shoulders, smoothed his mustache and waited for daybreak. Dawn arrived gradually through a swirling cloud of snowflakes that sparkled and bewildered the vision. Whatever portion of the landscape remained visible seemed mysteriously transformed. He gazed across the valley and captured their current situation and prospects in just two words—"snowed in!"

A thorough check of the supplies, which luckily for the group had been kept inside the cabin and therefore avoided Uncle Billy's thieving hands, revealed that with careful rationing they could stretch the food for another ten days. "That is," Mr. Oakhurst said quietly to the Innocent, "if you're willing to stay with us. If you're not—and maybe you shouldn't—you can wait until Uncle Billy comes back with more supplies." For some mysterious reason, Mr. Oakhurst couldn't bring himself to reveal Uncle Billy's betrayal, so instead he suggested that Uncle Billy had wandered away from camp and had accidentally spooked the animals into running off. He gave a subtle warning to the Duchess and Mother Shipton, who naturally knew the truth about their companion's abandonment. "They'll discover the truth about all of us when they discover anything," he added meaningfully, "and there's no point in scaring them right now."

Tom Simson not only offered all his worldly possessions to Mr. Oakhurst, but also seemed to relish the idea of their forced isolation. "We'll set up a great camp for a week, and then the snow will melt, and we'll all return together." The young man's cheerful enthusiasm, combined with Mr. Oakhurst's composure, spread to the others. The Innocent used pine branches to improvise a roof for the cabin that had none, while the Duchess guided Piney in reorganizing the interior with such skill and refinement that it made the country girl's blue eyes widen in amazement. "I suppose you're accustomed to elegant things back in Poker Flat," Piney remarked. The Duchess quickly turned away to hide something that brought color to her cheeks beneath her makeup, and Mother Shipton told Piney to stop her "chattering." However, when Mr. Oakhurst came back from an exhausting search for the trail, he heard the sound of joyful laughter echoing off the rocks. He paused with some concern, and his mind immediately went to the whisky he had wisely hidden away. "Yet somehow it doesn't sound like whisky," the gambler said to himself. Only when he glimpsed the bright fire through the still-blinding storm and saw the group gathered around it did he become convinced that it was genuine, innocent fun.

Whether Mr. Oakhurst had hidden his cards along with the whiskey as something forbidden from the community's free use, I cannot say. It was clear that, as Mother Shipton put it, he "didn't mention cards once" during that evening. Perhaps the time was made pleasant by an accordion, which Tom Simson pulled somewhat showily from his pack. Despite some challenges in playing this instrument, Piney Woods managed to coax several hesitant melodies from its keys, while the Innocent accompanied her on a pair of bone castanets. But the evening's greatest celebration came with a rough camp-meeting hymn, which the lovers sang with great seriousness and loud voices while holding hands. I suspect that a certain rebellious tone and Covenanter's rhythm in its chorus, rather than any religious quality, quickly spread to the others, who eventually joined in singing the refrain:

"I'm proud to live in service to the Lord."

"And I'm bound to die in His army."

The pine trees swayed back and forth, the storm swirled and spun above the wretched group, and the flames from their altar shot upward toward the sky as if marking their promise.

At midnight the storm calmed down, the rolling clouds separated, and the stars sparkled brightly above the sleeping camp. Mr. Oakhurst, whose work habits had allowed him to survive on very little sleep, somehow managed to take on most of the watch duty while sharing it with Tom Simson. He explained to the Innocent that he had "often gone a week without sleep." "Doing what?" Tom asked. "Poker!" Oakhurst replied briefly; "when a man hits a lucky streak— incredible luck—he doesn't get tired. The luck runs out first. Luck," the gambler continued thoughtfully, "is a very strange thing. All you know for sure about it is that it's bound to change. And figuring out when it's going to change is what makes or breaks you. We've had a run of bad luck since we left Poker Flat—you showed up, and suddenly you're caught up in it too. If you can play your cards right consistently, you'll be fine. Because," the gambler added with cheerful randomness,

"'I'm proud to live in the service of the Lord,

"And I'm bound to die in His army."

The third day arrived, and the sun, shining through the white-curtained valley, witnessed the outcasts dividing their slowly dwindling supply of food for breakfast. One of the unique characteristics of that mountain climate was how the sun's rays spread a gentle warmth across the winter landscape, as if offering sympathetic comfort for what had happened before. However, it also revealed pile after pile of snow heaped high around the cabin—a hopeless, unmapped, pathless ocean of white stretching below the rocky cliffs where the stranded group still held on. Through the remarkably clear air, smoke from the peaceful village of Poker Flat could be seen rising miles in the distance. Mother Shipton spotted it, and from a distant peak of her rocky stronghold, she hurled one final curse in that direction. This was her last angry outburst, and perhaps because of that, it carried a certain sense of dignity. It made her feel better, she privately told the Duchess. "Just go out there and curse, and you'll see what I mean." She then devoted herself to entertaining "the child," as she and the Duchess liked to call Piney. Piney wasn't exactly young, but it was a comforting and creative explanation the two women used to explain why she didn't curse and wasn't indecent.

When night crept up again through the gorges, the thin notes of the accordion rose and fell in irregular bursts and prolonged sighs beside the flickering campfire. But music couldn't completely fill the gnawing emptiness left by too little food, and Piney suggested a new distraction—telling stories. Since neither Mr. Oakhurst nor his female companions wanted to share their personal experiences, this idea would have failed as well if not for the Innocent. A few months earlier, he had stumbled across a stray copy of Mr. Pope's clever translation of the ILIAD. He now offered to tell the main events of that poem—having completely understood the plot while largely forgetting the exact words—using the everyday language of Sandy Bar. And so for the remainder of that night, the Homeric gods walked the earth once more. Trojan warriors and cunning Greeks battled in the winds, and the towering pines in the canyon appeared to bend before the fury of Peleus's son. Mr. Oakhurst listened with calm pleasure. He was particularly fascinated by the destiny of "Ash-heels," as the Innocent stubbornly continued to call the "swift-footed Achilles."

So with meager food supplies and plenty of Homer and the accordion, a week went by for the outcasts. The sun abandoned them once more, and snowflakes began falling again from gray, heavy skies across the landscape. Each day the snowy circle closed in tighter around them, until finally they gazed from their makeshift prison over towering walls of brilliant white snow that rose twenty feet above their heads. Finding fuel for their fires became increasingly challenging, even using the fallen trees nearby, which were now half-buried in the snowdrifts. Still, nobody voiced any complaints. The lovers turned away from the bleak view and gazed into each other's eyes, finding happiness there. Mr. Oakhurst calmly resigned himself to the losing hand he'd been dealt. The Duchess, showing more cheer than she had displayed before, took on the responsibility of caring for Piney. Only Mother Shipton—who had once been the strongest member of their group—appeared to grow weak and deteriorate. At midnight on the tenth day, she summoned Oakhurst to her side. "I'm dying," she told him, her voice frail and irritable, "but don't mention it to anyone. Don't wake the children. Take the bundle from beneath my head and unwrap it." Mr. Oakhurst followed her instructions. Inside he discovered Mother Shipton's food rations from the past week, completely untouched. "Give them to the girl," she said, gesturing toward the sleeping Piney. "You've been starving yourself," the gambler observed. "That's what people would call it," the woman replied irritably, as she lay back down and, turning her face toward the wall, quietly died.

The accordion and bones were set aside that day, and Homer was left unread. After Mother Shipton's body had been laid to rest in the snow, Mr. Oakhurst pulled the Innocent to one side and revealed a pair of snowshoes he had crafted from the old pack saddle. "There's still one chance in a hundred to save her," he said, gesturing toward Piney; "but it lies there," he continued, pointing in the direction of Poker Flat. "If you can make it there within two days, she'll be safe." "What about you?" Tom Simson asked. "I'm staying here," came the brief response.

The lovers separated with a lengthy embrace. "You're not leaving as well?" asked the Duchess when she noticed Mr. Oakhurst seemed to be waiting to go with him. "Just to the canyon," he answered. He turned abruptly and kissed the Duchess, leaving her pale face burning and her shaking limbs stiff with shock.

Night arrived, but Mr. Oakhurst did not return. The storm came back with swirling snow. When the Duchess was tending to the fire, she discovered that someone had silently stacked enough firewood next to the cabin to last several more days. Tears welled up in her eyes, but she concealed them from Piney.

The women barely slept at all. When morning came and they looked at each other's faces, they could see what lay ahead for them. Neither said a word, but Piney, taking on the role of the stronger one, moved closer and put her arm around the Duchess's waist. They stayed in this position for the remainder of the day. That night the storm reached its most violent peak, and tearing apart the protective pine trees, it broke into the hut itself.

As morning approached, they could no longer keep the fire burning, and it slowly went out. While the glowing coals gradually turned black, the Duchess moved closer to Piney and broke the silence that had lasted for hours: "Piney, are you able to pray?" "No, dear," Piney replied simply. The Duchess, though she couldn't say exactly why, felt a sense of relief, and resting her head on Piney's shoulder, said nothing more. Lying there together, with the younger and more innocent one cradling the head of her fallen companion against her pure chest, they drifted off to sleep.

The wind quieted as though it was afraid to disturb their sleep. Light, delicate snowflakes, shaken loose from the lengthy pine branches, drifted like birds with white wings and came to rest around them as they lay sleeping. The moon, shining through the broken clouds, gazed down at what had once been their campsite. But every mark of human presence, every sign of worldly struggle, was concealed beneath the pure white covering that had been compassionately cast down from the heavens.

They slept through that entire day and the following one, remaining unconscious even when voices and footsteps shattered the quiet of the camp. When compassionate hands gently swept the snow from their pale faces, it would have been nearly impossible to determine from the identical tranquility that rested upon them which one was the woman who had transgressed. Even the harsh justice of Poker Flat acknowledged this truth and withdrew, allowing them to remain forever embraced in each other's arms.

But at the top of the ravine, on one of the biggest pine trees, they discovered the two of clubs nailed to the bark with a hunting knife. It contained the following message, written in pencil with steady handwriting:

BENEATH THIS TREE
LIES THE BODY
OF
JOHN OAKHURST,
WHO HIT A STREAK OF BAD LUCK
ON NOVEMBER 23, 1850,
AND
HANDED IN HIS CHECKS
ON DECEMBER 7TH, 1850.

And lifeless and cold, with a Derringer beside him and a bullet through his heart, though still as peaceful as he had been in life, beneath the snow lay the man who was both the strongest and the weakest of all the outcasts from Poker Flat.

Miggles

We were eight people in total, counting the driver. None of us had spoken during the last six miles, since the heavy jolting of the stagecoach over the increasingly rough road had ruined the Judge's most recent poetical quote. The tall man sitting next to the Judge had fallen asleep, his arm threaded through the hanging strap with his head resting against it—he looked completely limp and helpless, as though he had hanged himself and been cut down too late. The French woman in the back seat was also asleep, though she maintained a half-conscious sense of proper posture, evident even in how she held the handkerchief against her forehead that partially covered her face. The woman from Virginia City, who was traveling with her husband, had long ago lost any trace of her individual appearance in a chaotic tangle of ribbons, veils, furs, and shawls. The only sounds were the clattering of wheels and rain pelting against the roof. All at once the stagecoach came to a halt, and we became vaguely aware of voices outside. The driver was clearly engaged in an animated conversation with someone on the road—a conversation from which we could occasionally make out fragments like "bridge gone," "twenty feet of water," and "can't pass" above the noise of the storm. Then there was a brief quiet, and a mysterious voice from the road called out a final warning:

"Try Miggles's."

We caught sight of our leaders as the wagon slowly turned, saw a rider disappearing through the rain, and it was clear we were heading to Miggles's place.

Who was Miggles and where could we find this person? The Judge, who served as our local expert, couldn't recall the name, even though he knew the area inside and out. The traveler from Washoe believed that Miggles must operate a hotel. All we knew for certain was that we found ourselves trapped by floodwaters both ahead and behind us, making Miggles our only hope for shelter. After ten minutes of splashing through a narrow, overgrown side road that was barely wide enough for our stagecoach, we pulled up in front of a gate that was barred and boarded shut, set within a broad stone wall or fence that stood about eight feet tall. This was clearly Miggles's place, and it was obvious that Miggles definitely did not run a hotel.

The driver climbed down and tested the gate. It was firmly locked. "Miggles! O Miggles!"

"Miggles! You Miggles!" the driver shouted, his anger growing stronger.

"Migglesy!" the delivery man chimed in, trying to persuade her. "Oh Miggy! Mig!"

But no response came from Miggles, who seemed completely unaware of their presence. The Judge, who had finally managed to get the window down, stuck his head out and asked a series of questions that, if answered directly, would have certainly cleared up the entire mystery, but the driver avoided giving straight answers by saying that "if we didn't want to sit in the coach all night, we had better get up and call out for Miggles."

So we got up and called out to Miggles all together, then one by one. After we were done, an Irish passenger from the roof shouted for "Maygells!" which made us all burst out laughing. While we were still laughing, the driver yelled "Shoo!"

We listened carefully. To our complete astonishment, the chorus of "Miggles" echoed back from the opposite side of the wall, including even the final and additional "Maygells."

"Extraordinary echo," said the Judge.

"What an absolutely despicable coward!" the driver shouted with contempt. "Get out here, Miggles, and show your face! Act like a man, Miggles! Don't cower there in the darkness; I certainly wouldn't if I were in your position, Miggles," Yuba Bill went on, now bouncing around in a fit of rage.

"Miggles!" the voice went on. "Oh Miggles!"

"My good man! Mr. Myghail!" said the Judge, making the harsh sounds of the name as gentle as he could. "Think about how unwelcoming it would be to refuse shelter from this terrible weather to helpless women. Really, my dear sir—" But a series of calls of "Miggles," ending in an explosion of laughter, drowned out his voice.

Yuba Bill didn't hesitate any longer. He picked up a heavy stone from the road and smashed down the gate, then entered the enclosure with the expressman. We followed behind them. No one was visible anywhere. In the growing darkness, all we could make out was that we had entered a garden—we could tell from the rosebushes that sprinkled us with tiny droplets from their wet leaves—and we stood before a long, sprawling wooden building.

"Do you know this Miggles?" the Judge asked Yuba Bill.

"No, and I don't want to," Bill said curtly, feeling that the Pioneer Stage Company had been insulted through him by the defiant Miggles.

"But, my dear sir," the Judge protested as he thought of the barred gate.

"Look here," said Yuba Bill, with sharp irony, "wouldn't you be better off going back to sit in the coach until you're properly introduced? I'm going inside," and he pushed open the door of the building.

A long room lit only by the glowing embers of a fire that was dying out in the large fireplace at the far end; the walls covered with unusual wallpaper, and the flickering firelight revealing its strange pattern; someone sitting in a large armchair beside the fireplace. We saw all of this as we pressed together into the room, following behind the driver and the delivery man.

"Hello, are you Miggles?" said Yuba Bill to the lone occupant.

The figure remained silent and motionless. Yuba Bill angrily approached it and directed the light from his coach lantern onto its face. It was a man's face, aged before its time and lined with wrinkles, featuring unusually large eyes that held an expression of completely unnecessary seriousness that I had occasionally observed in an owl's eyes. The large eyes shifted from Bill's face to the lantern, and eventually focused their stare on that glowing object, showing no other sign of awareness.

Bill held himself back with considerable effort.

"Miggles! Are you deaf? You're not mute anyway, you know"; and Yuba Bill shook the unconscious figure by the shoulder.

To our great dismay, when Bill pulled his hand away, the respected stranger seemed to collapse—shrinking to half his size and becoming an unrecognizable pile of clothes.

"Well, I'll be damned," said Bill, looking at us with a pleading expression and giving up on the argument completely.

The Judge stepped forward, and we carefully lifted the mysterious figure back to his original position. Bill was sent away with the lantern to scout the area outside, since it was clear that this helpless man couldn't be alone—there had to be other people nearby. We all gathered around the fire. The Judge, who had regained his commanding presence and never lost his charming way with words, stood before us with his back to the fireplace and addressed us as if we were a jury:

"It's clear that either our respected friend here has reached that state Shakespeare described as 'the sere and yellow leaf,' or he has experienced some early decline in his mental and physical abilities. Whether he is truly the Miggles—"

At that moment, he was cut off by cries of "Miggles! Oh Miggles! Migglesy! Mig!" and indeed, the entire chorus of voices calling for Miggles rang out in much the same tone as we had heard it delivered to us once before.

We stared at each other for a moment, feeling quite alarmed. The Judge, especially, moved away from his spot quickly, since the voice seemed to come from right behind him. However, we soon found the source of the sound—a large magpie sitting on a shelf above the fireplace, who immediately fell back into a deathly quiet that was strikingly different from his earlier chattiness. Without a doubt, it was his voice we had heard from the road, and our friend sitting in the chair wasn't to blame for the rude behavior. Yuba Bill, who came back into the room after searching unsuccessfully, was reluctant to believe this explanation and continued to look at the helpless man with distrust. He had found a shed where he could shelter his horses, but he returned soaking wet and doubtful. "There ain't nobody but him within ten miles of this cabin, and that damned old troublemaker knows it."

But most people's confidence turned out to be well-founded. Bill had barely stopped growling when we heard quick footsteps on the porch, the sound of a wet dress dragging, the door burst open, and a young woman rushed in with gleaming white teeth, sparkling dark eyes, and complete lack of formality or shyness, slammed the door behind her, and leaned back against it, breathing heavily.

"Oh, if you please, I'm Miggles!"

And this was Miggles! This bright-eyed, full-voiced young woman, whose soaked dress of rough blue fabric couldn't conceal the beauty of her feminine figure that it hugged; from the chestnut crown of her head, topped with a man's waterproof rain hat, down to her small feet and ankles, hidden somewhere deep inside her boy's heavy shoes, everything about her was graceful—this was Miggles, laughing at us as well, in the most lighthearted, honest, casual way you could imagine.

"You see, boys," she said, completely out of breath and pressing one small hand against her side, paying no attention to the speechless embarrassment of our group or the total confusion of Yuba Bill, whose face had softened into an expression of pointless and foolish cheerfulness—"you see, boys, I was more than two miles away when you passed down the road. I thought you might stop here, so I ran the entire way, knowing nobody was home except Jim,—and—and—I'm out of breath—and—that's all I can manage."

And at that moment Miggles pulled her soaking wet oilskin hat from her head with a playful twist that sent a spray of raindrops flying over us; she tried to smooth back her hair; lost two hairpins in the process; burst into laughter and settled down next to Yuba Bill, folding her hands gently in her lap.

The Judge was the first to regain his composure, and he attempted an elaborate compliment.

"I'll need that hairpin back," said Miggles seriously. Several hands quickly reached forward; the lost hairpin was returned to its rightful owner; and Miggles, walking across the room, looked intently into the invalid's face. The serious eyes gazed back at hers with an expression we had never witnessed before. Life and awareness appeared to fight their way back into the weathered face. Miggles laughed again—it was a remarkably expressive laugh—and turned her dark eyes and bright teeth toward us once more.

"This troubled person is—" the Judge hesitated.

"Jim," said Miggles.

"Your father?"

"No."

"Brother?"

"No."

"Husband?"

Miggles shot a quick, somewhat defiant look at the two female passengers who I had observed weren't joining in with the men's general admiration of Miggles, and said seriously, "No; it's Jim."

There was an uncomfortable silence. The female passengers huddled closer together; the Washoe husband stared blankly at the fire; and the tall man seemed to look within himself for strength during this crisis. But Miggles's laughter, which was quite contagious, shattered the quiet. "Come on," she said energetically, "you all must be starving. Who's going to lend me a hand with preparing tea?"

She had plenty of volunteers. Within moments, Yuba Bill was working like Caliban carrying logs for this Miranda;

the expressman was grinding coffee on the veranda; I was given the demanding task of slicing bacon; and the Judge offered each person his cheerful and talkative advice. And when Miggles, helped by the Judge and our Irish "deck passenger," set the table with all the dishes they could find, we had become quite cheerful, despite the rain beating against the windows, the wind swirling down the chimney, the two ladies whispering together in the corner, or the magpie making sarcastic and harsh comments on their conversation from his perch above. In the now bright, roaring fire we could see that the walls were covered with illustrated magazines, arranged with feminine taste and careful selection. The furniture was improvised and made from candle boxes and packing crates, covered with colorful calico or animal skins. The armchair for helpless Jim was a clever adaptation of a flour barrel. There was tidiness, and even an appreciation for beauty, visible in the few details of the long, low room.

The meal was a culinary success. But more than that, it was a social triumph—mainly, I believe, due to Miggles's exceptional skill in directing the conversation, asking all the questions herself, while maintaining a straightforwardness that dismissed any notion of hiding anything on her part, so that we discussed ourselves, our future plans, the trip, the weather, each other—everything except our host and hostess. It must be admitted that Miggles's conversation was never refined, seldom grammatically correct, and that sometimes she used curse words that had typically been reserved for our gender. But these were delivered with such a brightening of teeth and eyes, and were usually accompanied by a laugh—a laugh unique to Miggles—so genuine and sincere that it seemed to cleanse the moral atmosphere.

Once during the meal we heard a noise like the rubbing of a heavy body against the outer walls of the house. This was shortly followed by a scratching and sniffing at the door. "That's Joaquin," said Miggles, responding to our questioning looks; "would you like to see him?" Before we could answer she had opened the door, and revealed a half-grown grizzly bear, who immediately raised himself on his hind legs, with his front paws hanging down in the familiar pose of begging, and looked admiringly at Miggles, with a very striking resemblance in his behavior to Yuba Bill. "That's my watchdog," said Miggles, by way of explanation. "Oh, he doesn't bite," she added, as the two lady passengers fluttered into a corner. "Do you, old Toppy?" (this last comment being directed straight to the clever Joaquin). "I tell you what, boys," continued Miggles after she had fed him and closed the door on the little bear, "you were really lucky that Joaquin wasn't hanging around when you showed up tonight." "Where was he?" asked the Judge. "With me," said Miggles. "Good Lord; he follows me around at night just like he was a person."

We stayed quiet for a few minutes, listening to the wind. Maybe we were all imagining the same thing—Miggles walking through the rainy forest with her fierce protector beside her. The Judge, I recall, made some comment about Una and her lion, but Miggles accepted it the way she received all compliments, with calm seriousness. I don't know whether she was completely unaware of the admiration she stirred up—she could hardly have missed Yuba Bill's devotion—but her straightforward manner suggested a complete sexual equality that was painfully embarrassing to the younger men in our group.

The bear incident didn't improve Miggles's standing with the women who witnessed it. After the meal ended, the two female passengers radiated such coldness that even the pine branches Yuba Bill gathered and threw onto the fire as an offering couldn't completely dispel the chill. Miggles sensed their disapproval, and abruptly announced it was time to "turn in," offering to escort the ladies to their sleeping quarters in the next room. "You boys will have to make camp here by the fire however you can manage," she said, "since there's only one bedroom."

Our gender—by which, my dear sir, I naturally refer to the stronger half of humanity—has typically been spared accusations of being curious or having a taste for gossip. However, I must admit that the moment the door shut behind Miggles, we huddled together, whispering, chuckling, grinning, and sharing suspicions, theories, and countless speculations about our attractive hostess and her unusual companion. I'm afraid we even jostled that helpless paralyzed man, who sat like a silent Memnon among us, watching our animated discussions with the calm detachment of ages past reflected in his intense eyes. Right in the middle of our heated conversation, the door opened once more, and Miggles came back in.

But this wasn't the same Miggles who had appeared before us just a few hours earlier. Her gaze was lowered, and as she paused briefly at the doorway with a blanket draped over her arm, she appeared to have abandoned the open boldness that had captivated us moments before. Entering the room, she pulled a small stool next to the paralyzed man's chair, settled down, wrapped the blanket around her shoulders, and said, "If you don't mind, boys, since we're pretty cramped in here, I'll stay here tonight." She took the sick man's frail hand in hers and fixed her gaze on the fading fire. An intuitive sense that this was just the beginning of more intimate conversations, and perhaps some embarrassment about our earlier nosiness, kept us quiet. The rain continued pounding on the roof, occasional wind gusts stirred the coals into brief flashes of light, until, during a break in the storm, Miggles suddenly raised her head, and sweeping her hair back over her shoulder, turned to face our group and asked:

"Is there anyone among you who knows me?"

There was no reply.

"Think again! I lived in Marysville back in '53. Everyone knew me there, and everyone had every right to know me. I ran the Polka saloon until I moved in with Jim. That was six years ago. Maybe I've changed somewhat."

The lack of recognition might have unsettled her. She turned her head back toward the fire, and several seconds passed before she spoke again, this time more quickly:

"Well, you see, I thought some of you must have known me. There's no real harm done, anyway. What I was going to say was this: Jim here"—she took his hand in both of hers as she spoke—"used to know me, if you didn't, and spent a lot of money on me. I think he spent everything he had. And one day—it's six years ago this winter—Jim came into my back room, sat down on my sofa, just like you see him in that chair, and never moved again without help. He was completely overwhelmed, and never seemed to understand what was wrong with him. The doctors came and said that it was caused entirely by his lifestyle—because Jim was very reckless and wild—and that he would never get better, and couldn't live long anyway. They advised me to send him to San Francisco to the hospital, because he was no use to anyone and would be like a child for the rest of his life. Perhaps it was something in Jim's eyes, perhaps it was because I never had a baby, but I said 'No.' I was wealthy then, because I was well-liked by everyone—

gentlemen like yourself, sir, came to see me—and I sold my business and bought this place, because it was somewhat off the beaten path, you see, and I brought my baby here."

With a woman's natural intuition and grace, she had gradually moved while speaking, positioning herself so that the silent figure of the broken man stood between her and those watching. She retreated into the shadow behind him, as though presenting him as an unspoken explanation for what she had done. Though he remained quiet and showed no emotion, he seemed to speak on her behalf; despite being powerless, defeated, and struck down by God's judgment, he still seemed to wrap a protective arm around her that no one could see.

Hidden in the darkness, but still holding his hand, she continued:

"It took me a long time to figure out how to manage things around here, since I was accustomed to having company and excitement around me. I couldn't find any woman to assist me, and I didn't dare trust a man with the work; but between the local Indians who would take on small jobs for me, and having all our supplies shipped in from North Fork, Jim and I somehow managed to get by. The Doctor would come up from Sacramento from time to time. He would ask to see 'Miggles's baby,' which is what he called Jim, and when he was ready to leave, he would say, 'Miggles, you're a gem—God bless you'; and things didn't feel quite so isolated after his visits. But the last time he came here, as he opened the door to leave, he said, 'Do you know, Miggles, your baby is going to grow up to be a man someday and make his mother proud; but not here, Miggles, not here!' And I felt like he left feeling sad—and—and—" and at this point both Miggles's voice and her head seemed to disappear entirely into the shadows.

"The people around here are very kind," said Miggles, after a pause, stepping a little into the light again. "The men from the fork used to hang around here, until they realized they weren't wanted, and the women are kind—and don't visit. I was pretty lonely until I found Joaquin in the woods over there one day, when he wasn't so tall, and taught him to beg for his dinner; and then there's Polly—that's the magpie—she knows countless tricks, and makes it quite companionable in the evenings with her chatter, so I don't feel like I'm the only living creature around the ranch. And Jim here," said Miggles, with her old laugh again, and stepping out completely into the firelight, "Jim—why, boys, you would be amazed to see how much he understands for a man like him. Sometimes I bring him flowers, and he looks at them just as naturally as if he recognized them; and sometimes, when we're sitting alone, I read him those things on the wall. Why, Lord!" said Miggles, with her honest laugh, "I've read him that entire side of the house this winter. There never was such a man for listening to reading as Jim."

"Why," the Judge asked, "don't you marry this man to whom you've dedicated your young life?"

"Well, you see," said Miggles, "it would be taking unfair advantage of Jim to exploit his helpless condition. And besides, if we were husband and wife, we'd both understand that I'd be obligated to do what I now choose to do willingly."

"But you're still young and attractive—"

"It's getting late," Miggles said seriously, "and you should all go to bed. Good night, boys." She pulled the blanket over her head and lay down next to Jim's chair, resting her head on the low stool that supported his feet, then said nothing more. The fire gradually died down in the fireplace; we all quietly found our blankets; and soon the

33

only sounds in the long room were the drumming of rain on the roof and the deep breathing of those who slept.

I woke up near dawn from a restless dream. The storm had ended, stars were gleaming, and the full moon rose above the towering pines outside, casting its light through the window that had no shutters. The moonlight touched the solitary figure sitting in the chair with endless tenderness, and appeared to bless with its brilliant glow the bowed head of the woman whose hair, like in that beautiful ancient tale, had washed the feet of the man she cherished. The gentle light even gave a touching grace to Yuba Bill's rough silhouette as he lay propped up on his elbow between them and his passengers, his fierce yet patient eyes standing guard through the night. Then I drifted back to sleep and didn't wake again until full daylight, with Yuba Bill looming over me and the call of "All aboard" echoing in my ears.

Coffee was waiting for us on the table, but Miggles had disappeared. We walked around the house and stayed much longer than we should have after the horses were ready to go, but she never came back. It was clear that she wanted to avoid saying goodbye formally, and had left us to go on our way just as we had arrived. After we had helped the women into the coach, we went back to the house and seriously shook hands with paralyzed Jim, carefully helping him settle back into his position after each handshake. Then we took one final look around the long, low room, at the stool where Miggles had been sitting, and slowly got into the waiting coach. The whip snapped, and we were on our way!

But when we reached the main road, Bill's skillful hand pulled the six horses back onto their hind legs, and the stagecoach came to an abrupt stop. There, standing on a small hill next to the road, was Miggles with her hair blowing in the wind, her eyes bright and lively, her white handkerchief waving, and her white teeth gleaming as she called out one final "goodbye." We waved our hats back at her. Then Yuba Bill, as though afraid of being charmed any further, frantically whipped his horses forward, and we settled back into our seats. We didn't speak a single word to each other until we arrived at the North Fork, where the stagecoach pulled up in front of the Independence House. At that point, with the Judge leading the way, we entered the barroom and solemnly took our positions at the bar.

"Are your glasses filled, gentlemen?" asked the Judge, ceremoniously removing his white hat.

They were.

"Well, then, here's to MIGGLES. GOD BLESS HER!"

Perhaps He had. Who knows?

THE END

Thank You For Reading

You've Just Read a Piece of the Greatest Library Ever Rebuilt

Thank you for reading.

This book is one of thousands we're restoring, reimagining, and translating as part of the **Modern Library of Alexandria** — a global movement to preserve and share humanity's most important ideas.

What was once lost to fire and time is now rising again — not just as memory, but as living, breathing knowledge, freely accessible to all.

What You Can Do Next:

* **Keep Reading.**

    Discover more legendary works — in beautiful print, audiobook, or digital form — at LibraryofAlexandria.com.

* **Build Your Own Library.**

    Every title is available as a paperback, hardcover, or collectible boxset — at true printing cost. Craft a personal library worthy of display.

* **Spread the Light.**

    Share this book. Tell others about the movement. Help us translate every timeless work into every language, so no reader is ever left behind.

By finishing this book, you've already taken part in something extraordinary.

Join us at LibraryofAlexandria.com

Together, we're rebuilding the greatest library the world has ever known.

With appreciation,

The Modern Library of Alexandria Team

Visit:
www.libraryofalexandria.com
Or scan the code below: